六祖坛经

WISDOM OF THE ZEN MASTERS

曹·溪·的·佛·唱
The Quest For Enlightenment

蔡志忠/著　BRIAN BRUYA(美)/译

蔡志忠漫画中英文版

现代出版社

Contents

Translatar's Preface	1
Transmission of the Lamp	1
The Quest For Enlightenment	3
The Sixth Patriarch Huineng	15
A Special Transmission Apart From the Scriptures	29
Not Reliant On Language	30
Direct Pointing At One's Mind	31
Seeing One's Nature, Becoming a Buddha	32
Non-Abiding	33
Sudden In the South, Gradual In the North	34
Huairang Of Nanyue	35
Xingsi Of Qingyuan	37
Xuanjue Of Yongjia	39
Huizhong Of Nanyang	42
Shenhui Of Heze	44
Dayi, Patriarch Ma (Mazu)	48
Seeking a Mule While Riding a Mule	51
The Hunter's Marksmanship	52
Self-Nature	54
How Could It Have Flown Away	56
Buddha Of the Sun, Buddha Of the Moon	57
Zen Of the Wild Fox	58
Baizhang's Regulations	60
A Day Without Work, A Day Without Food	62
The Fire In the Embers	63
The Great Suppression	64
Xiangyan Hits Bamboo	66
The Mind Is the Buddha	68
The Devil Of Language	69

Eating And Sleeping	71	Chongxin Of Longtan	86
Self And Other	72	The Bodhisattva Shanhui	88
Congshen of Zhaozhou	73	Standing For the Emperor	89
Nanquan Kills a Cat	75	Three Schools In One	90
Kicked By a Donkey	76	Shanhui's Zen Poem	91
Not a Stitch On	78	Liangjie Of Dongshan	92
The Dao Is In Dung	79	Fayan Wenyi	96
If the Mind Is Pure, Everything Is Pure	80	A Drop Of Water From the Cao River	98
The Buddha-Nature Of a Dog	81	Emptiness	99
Dust	82	Wenyan Of Yunmen	100
Zhen Prefecture's Big White Radishes	83	Everyday Is a Good Day	102
Daowu Of Tianhuang	84	One Word Gate	103
		Yunmen's Three Lines	104

Translator's Preface

Tsai Chih Chung (C. C. Tsai, for short) is the most accomplished and popular cartoonist in all of East Asia, with some of his books even being incorporated into the public school curriculum in Japan. C. C. Tsai began his career at the age of sixteen by publishing the first of what would be approximately 200 swashbuckler comic books. Following that, he went into animation and garnered himself the equivalent of our Oscar while building up the largest animation company in Taiwan. In his spare time, he turned to the humor of comic strips and put out the first daily comic strip in Taiwan newspapers.

One day on a flight to Japan, he began to sketch scenes from a book he was reading. The book had been written over two thousand years ago by a famous Daoist (Taoist) thinker named Zhuangzi (Chuang Tsu). From these sketches emerged a new genre in the book world — a serious (though light-hearted) comic book explicating a topic. C. C.'s aim was not to simplify, but to clarify. The ancient language in China is difficult for modern people to understand, so in addition to illustrating the subject matter, he also rendered the text into

Modern Chinese.

When *Zhuangzi Speaks* came out in Taiwan, it shot to the top of the bestseller list, and the head of a major publishing company immediately remarked that it had world potential. Tired of animation by now, C. C. sold off his company and devoted all of his efforts to the daily comic strips and his new series on ancient Chinese thought, both of which were bringing him unparalleled fame for a cartoonist. Soon, he held the four highest spots atop the bestseller list, until other authors demanded that comic books no longer be allowed on the list of serious literature. The publishers of the list acquiesced. Undaunted, C. C. went on researching, illustrating, and publishing. There are now over twenty in the series and millions of copies in print, and they are rapidly gaining popularity all over the world.

Zen Masters of Old, as the title suggests, is about Zen Buddhism, which is more of an attitude toward life than a system of strict religious belief. The episodes within are for the most part short dialogues between various well-known Zen masters and their students. Most are drawn directly from pre-modern Zen literature, such books as the *Platform Sutra of the Sixth Patriarch*, the *Transmission of the Lamp*, the *Gateless Gate (Mumonkan)*, and the Blue *Cliff Record*. C. C. translated the laconic Classical Chinese into highly readable yet technically accurate Modern Chinese, which I have done my best to render into familiar, idiomatic English, taking care not to oversimplify.

Often you will see a monk referred to as "such and such a monk from such and such a place," for instance, "Congshen of Zhaozhou". Then later you will see him referred to as Zhaozhou. It may seem odd to see a monk referred to solely by his place of origin but it arose out of the practice of putting the place-name first when referring to someone. For instance, Congshen of Zhaozhou was called Zhaozhou Congshen, and as time went by and his name was repeated over and over, the end was dropped off, leaving only "Zhaozhou". It is commom in this book, but of course, it only happened for the most well-known monks. It is similar to us referring to John Fitzgerald Kennedy as J.F.K.. Now, the initials "J.F.K." could refer to numerous people, but we have repeated his name so many times that this simple reduction works to identify him.

You'll also notice that for dates, I translate for instance, "the ninth month", rather than "September". The reason for this is that the Chinese then used a lunar calendar, in which case the 9th month could correspond to our September or October, depending on the year. Notice that even now the Chinese "New Year" isn't celebrated until late January or early February.

In regard to the Chinese at the margin of each page, it is retained nominally for reference purposes, as it contains the original text in some places and notes thrown in by the original Chinese editor in other places. More to the point, it's a nice decorative touch; don't get the idea that your are missing out on any essential information.

I hope you enjoy reading *Zen Masters of Old* as much as I have enjoyed translating it.

—B. B.

曹溪的佛唱——《六祖坛经》

本来无一物，何处惹尘埃。
菩提本无树，明镜亦非台；

言：「汝但诵偈，吾为汝书。」慧能偈曰："欲学无上菩提，不得轻于初学。下下人有上上智，上上人有没意智，若轻人，即有无量无边罪。"别驾言："汝亦作偈，其事希有。"慧能向别驾言：读，慧能闻已，遂言："亦有一偈，望别驾为书。"别驾言："童子引至偈前礼拜，慧能曰："慧能不识字，请上人为读。"时有江州别驾，姓张名日用，便高声

《景德传灯录》

Wisdom has never been a tree
And the bright mirror has no stand
There has never been anything
So whereupon can the dust land

Zen Masters Of Old
The Quest For Enlightenment

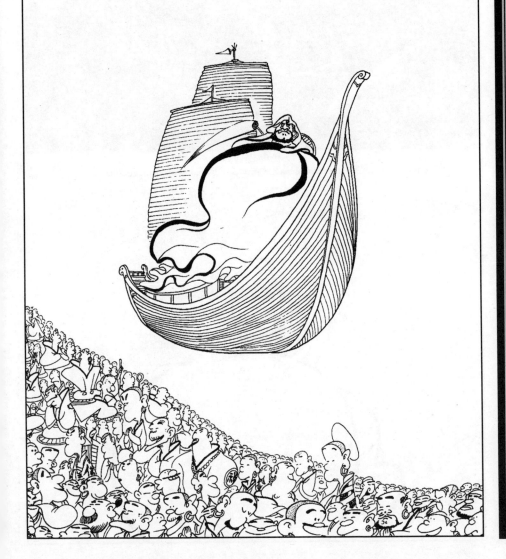

尊者曰：「汝所化之方，获菩提者不可胜数，吾灭后六十余年，彼国有难，水中文布，自善降之，汝至设大法药，直接上根，慎勿速行，衰于日下。」师又曰：「彼有大士堪为法器否？千载之下有留难否？」而作佛事？愿垂开示。」尊者曰：「汝虽得法，未可远游，且止南天竺，待吾灭后六十七载，当往震旦得通量，夫达摩者，通大之义也，宜名达摩，因改号菩提达摩。」师乃告尊者曰：「我既得法，当往何国多罗至本国受王供养，知师密迹，因试令与二兄辨所施宝珠，发明心要。既而尊者谓曰：「汝于诸法已第二十八祖菩提达摩者，南天竺国香至王第三子也，姓刹帝利，本名菩提多罗，后遇二十七祖般若

曹溪的佛唱——六祖坛经

曹溪的佛昌——六祖云云

八年丁未岁九月二十一日也。毕早回。」王闻师言，王即具大舟，实以众宝，躬率臣察，送至海壖，师泛重溟，凡三周寒暑，达于南海，实梁普通回。」王闻师言，涕泪交集。曰：「此国何罪？彼土何祥？叔既有缘，非吾所止，惟愿不忘父母之国，事乃至辞祖塔，次别同学。然至王所，慰而勉之。曰：「当勤修白业，护持三宝，吾去非晚，一九即（中略）时，南方勿往，彼惟好有为功业，不见佛理。汝纵到彼，亦不可久留。」……

In the year 527, the first year of the Datong reign of the Liang dynasty...

A monk from India named Bodhidharma arrived at the shores of southern China.

4

曹溪的佛昌——六祖云□

无上妙道，旷劫精勤，难行能行，非忍而忍，岂以小德小智轻心慢心欲冀真乘，徒劳勤苦。」光闻师诲问曰：「诸佛崖伺虎，古尚若此，我又何人？」其年十二月九日夜，天大雨雪。光坚立不动，迟明积雪过膝。师悯而问曰：「汝久立雪中，当求何事？」光悲泪曰：「惟愿和尚慈悲，开甘露门，广度群品。」师曰：「昔人求道，敲骨取髓，刺血济饥，布发掩泥，投彼晨夕参承，师常端坐面墙，莫闻诲励。光自惟曰：「孔老之教，礼术风规，庄易之书，未尽妙理，近闻达摩大士住止少林，至人不遥，当造玄境，每叹曰：莫之测，谓之壁观婆罗门。时有僧神光者，旷达之士也，久居伊洛，博览群书，善谈玄理，

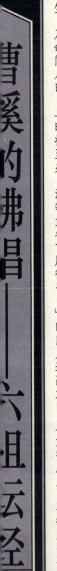

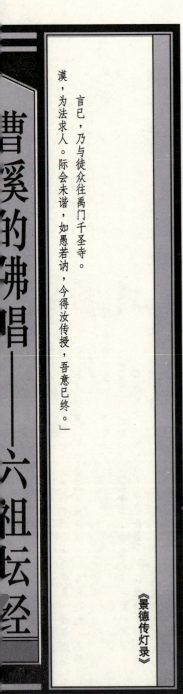

曹溪的佛唱——六祖坛经

第三祖僧璨大师者，不知何许人也，初以白衣谒二祖，既受度传法，隐于舒州之皖公山，属后周武帝破灭佛法。师往来太湖县司空山，居无常处，积十余载，时人无能知者。至隋开皇十二年壬子岁，有沙弥道信，年始十四，来礼师曰：「愿和尚慈悲，乞与解脱法门。」师曰：「谁缚汝？」曰：「无人缚。」师曰：「何更求解脱乎？」信于言下大悟，服劳九载，后于吉州受戒，侍奉尤谨，师屡试以玄微，知其缘熟，乃付衣法。偈曰：华种虽生地，从地种华生；若无人下种，华地尽无生。

《景德传灯录》

曹溪的佛唱——六祖坛经

曹溪的佛唱——六祖坛经

师遂辞去，直造黄梅之东禅。即唐咸亨二年也。师遂请益。远曰：「观子神姿爽拔，殆非常人，吾闻西域菩提达摩，传心印于黄梅，汝当往彼参决。」明日遂行，至昌乐县，西山石室间，遇智远禅师，于是，居人竞来瞻礼。近有宝林古寺旧地，众议营缉，俾师居之，四众雾集，俄成宝坊。能曰：「诸佛理论，若取文字，非佛意也。」尼深叹服，号为行者。师一日忽自念曰：「我求大法，岂可中道而止。」咸亨中往韶阳，遇刘志略，略有姑，无尽藏，恒读《涅槃经》，能听之，即为尼辨析中义。怪能不识文字。《高僧传》

True geniuses are not of this world. The sixth patriarch Huineng was this kind of genius. He, Laozi (Lao-tzu), Zhuangzi (Chuang-tzu), Confucius, and Mencius were great men of the same strain.

His thinking, his words, and his actions were compiled by disciples into a short book called the Platform Sūtra of the Sixth Patriarch, the only Chinese Buddhist work to attain the status of a sacred scripture.

The Platform Sūtra is a heartfelt book generated by a truly genuine person. Every word, every sentence, is as fresh and penetrating as water from a clear spring.

曹溪的弗唱——《六祖坛经》

至后院。有一行者，差慧能破柴踏碓，八月余日。祖一日忽唤慧能，曰：「吾思汝之见可用，恐有恶人害汝，遂不与汝言，汝知之否？」慧能曰：「弟子亦知师意，不敢行至堂前，令人不觉。」祖一日唤诸门人总来：「吾向汝说，世人生死事大，汝等终日只求福田，不求出离生死苦海，自性若迷，福何可救？汝等各去，自看智慧，取自本心般若之性，各作一偈，来呈吾看。若悟大意，付汝衣法，为第六代祖。火急速去，不得迟滞，思量即不中用。见性之人，言下须见，若如此者，轮刀上阵，亦得见之。」

《六祖坛经》

6. Abiding in nothing, let thy mind come through...

7. Excuse me, what Sūtra is that you're quoting? / The Diamond Sūtra.

8. Where did you study the Buddhist scriptures? / I studied with the fifth patriarch Hongren at Huangmei Mountain in Hebei.

9. Huineng then put his mother under the care of a neighbor,

10. And departed for Hebei to study the buddha-dharma...

11. After 30 days of walking, he arrived at Huangmei, whereupon he immediately went to meet Hongren. / Where are you from, and why are you here?

曹溪的弗唱——六祖坛经

人尽来，焚香偈前，令众人见，皆生敬心：「汝等尽诵此，悟此偈者，方得见性；依此修行，即不堕神秀上座，题此偈毕，归卧房，并无人见。五祖平旦，于南廊下，忽见此偈请记，（中略）遂唤门时时勤拂拭，莫使惹尘埃。身是菩提树，心如明镜台；间壁上，秉烛题作偈，人尽不知，偈曰：甚难。夜至三更，不令人见，遂向南廊下，中间壁上，题作呈心偈。（中略）秀上座三更于南廊下，中

Among Hongren's disciples, one Shenxiu was recognized by all to be the one most likely to receive the robe and almsbowl.

The body is the wisdom tree,
The mind like a bright mirror stand;
Always strive to wipe it clean,
Making sure that no dust lands.

……

Wonderful. Yes.

Fantastic.

The body is the wisdom tree, The mind like a bright mirror stand; Always strive to wipe it clean, Making sure that no dust lands!

!

Who wrote that?

Shenxiu. He wrote it on the wall.

Can you take me to see it?

OK.

The body is the wisdom tree, The mind like a bright mirror stand; Always strive to wipe it clean, Making sure that no dust lands.

Here it is.

Oh.

曹溪的佛唱——六祖坛经

日，作不得。
性。汝且去，一两日来，思惟，更作一偈来呈吾，若得入门，见自本性，当付汝衣法。」秀上座去数日，作不得。
前，尚未得入。凡夫依此偈修行，即不堕落。作此见解，若觅无上菩提，即未可得，须得入门，见自本性。愿和尚慈悲，看弟子有小智慧，识大意否？」五祖曰：「汝作此偈，见即未到，只到门前，尚未得入。凡夫依此偈修行，即不堕落。」（中略）
五祖遂唤秀上座于堂内，问：「是汝作偈否？若是汝作，应得我法。」秀上座言：「罪过，实是秀作，不敢求祖。愿和尚慈悲，看弟子有小智慧，识大意否？」

《六祖坛经》

书此偈已，徒众总惊，无不嗟讶！各相谓言：「奇哉！不得以貌取人，何得多时，使他肉身菩萨。」

菩提本无树，明镜亦非台；本来无一物，何处惹尘埃。

罪。」别驾言：「欲学无上菩提，不得轻于初学。下下人有上上智，上上人有没意智，若轻人，即有无量无边罪。」慧能偈曰：

言：「汝但诵偈，吾为汝书。」慧能言：「亦有一偈，望别驾为书。」别驾言：「汝亦作偈，其事希有。」慧能向别驾

读，慧能闻已，遂言：

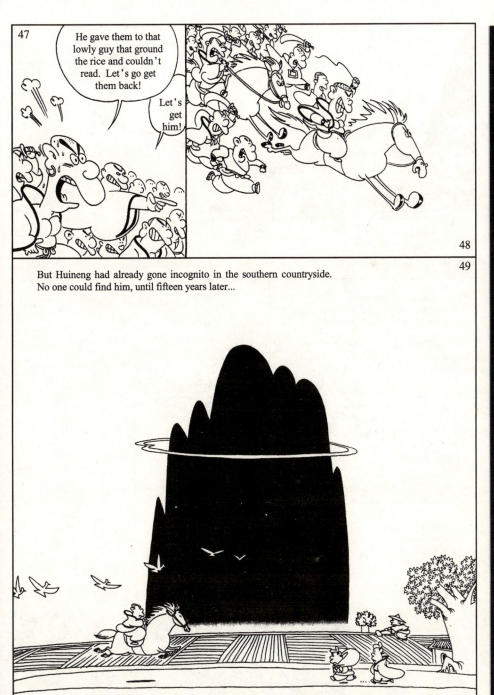

曹溪的弗昌——六祖坛经

然返曹溪，两大法雨，学者不下千数。时韶州刺史韦据，请于大梵寺转妙法轮，并受无相心地戒。明年二月八日，师忽谓众曰：「吾不愿此居，要归旧隐。」时印宗与缁白千余人，送师归宝林寺。（中略）师具戒已，于此开东山法门。（中略）至正月十五日，会诸名德，为之剃发。二月八日，就法性寺智光律师，受满分戒。其戒坛即宋朝求那跋陀三藏所置也。出所传信衣，悉令瞻礼。

《景德传灯录》

---

61 I heard that Hongren's robe and almsbowl were transmitted south. You aren't the one who received them are you?

62 That's right.

63 Wow!

64 Your disciples seek guidance from the sixth patriarch!

65 Following this, Yinzong shaved Huineng's head and formally ordained him.

66 And then he himself took Huineng as his teacher.

67 The following year, Huineng went to the area near the Cao river and, through the support of his many followers, constructed Baolin monastery. It was here that he began spreading the dharma.

且将经典的真髓以自己的言词直接地表现出来。表现并不局限于传统的佛教学，这或许是基于从踏碓或卖薪所得的伟大体验。他不仅不为经典所局限，说，比起向他人说禅，显得更重视经典或解释。与此相反，慧能精通《涅槃经》，也很有学问，可是其五祖弘忍门下的北宗神秀，是一杰出的人物，也是一位学解相应的禅者。但看其《北宗五方便》之

引自康华编著《中国禅》

曹溪的佛唱——六祖坛经

曹溪的佛唱——六祖云圣

目标就是动。他说：「各位，我在弘忍和尚处所以听了一句话就大悟，乃由于能顿见真如本性。」动作即见、看即静、见即动。所以慧能所持的态度来看，并以实体化来凝视。相反的，慧能的禅就是「见」，而见就是「认识」。见是要以动制物，而非看净。所谓「看」，就是凝视某一物之意，亦即将物视为静止。他认为「佛性」就是将佛性以静止状四祖道信或五祖弘忍的东山法门之禅，是注重「守心」、「看心」，然而慧能的坐禅并非看心，也

引自康华编著《中国禅》

68
Not reliant on language
A special transmission apart from the scriptures
Direct pointing at one's heart
Seeing one's nature, becoming a buddha.

Using these four lines to describe Bodhidharma's thought would be correct, but they would be so much more accurate in describing Huineng's thinking.

69
The way of perfect wisdom is mind to mind transmission, whereas books and scriptures are just a convenient method of opening one's mind toward self-enlightenment.

70
Even the wisest of all teachers cannot stuff his own enlightenment into another person's mind. He can only act like a midwife and wait for the right time to lend a helping hand.

曹溪的佛唱——《六祖坛经》

「本心。」

《菩萨戒经》云：「我本元自性清净。」识心见性，自成佛道。《维摩经》云：「即时豁然，还得本心，即是佛是众生；一念若悟，即众生是佛。故知：一切万法，尽在自身中，何不从于自心顿现真如本性，即是佛是众生；迷人若悟解心开，与大智人无别。故知：不悟，佛是众生；一念若悟，即众生是佛。故知万法本因人兴，一切经书，因人说有。缘在人中有愚有智；愚为小人，智为大人；迷人问于智者，智人与愚人说法。令彼愚者悟解心解。迷人若悟解心开，与大智人无别。故知：本心不有。故知万法本因人兴，一切经书及诸文字，小大二乘，十二部经，皆因人置，因智惠性故，故然能建立，若无世人，一切万法，本元不有。」

《六祖坛经》

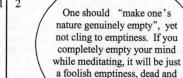

Huairang Of Nanyue
(677 ~ 744)

From Jin prefecture in Shaanxi province, his lay surname was Du. He left his family for the order at fifteen and first studied the Vinaya Sect. Unsatisfied, however, he went to Song Mountain to study under Huaian, who suggested he go to Caoxi (Cao river) to study under Huineng.

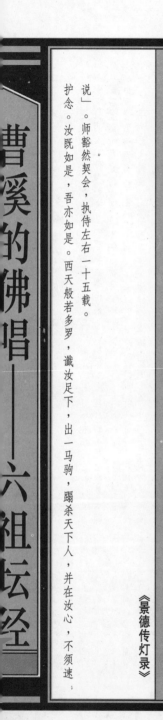

Xingsi Of Qingyuan
(660 ~ 740)

From Ji prefecture in Jiangxi province, his lay surname was Liu. He left home to join the order at a very young age and he was of a quiet disposition.

1. At his first meeting with Huineng, he asked: What can we do to keep from slipping into the levels of relativism?

2. What works have you done lately?

3. I haven't even worked on the sacred truth.

4. And what level has this work brought you to?

5. If I haven't even worked on the sacred truth, what level is there to speak of? Good, good. Very good.

6. Huineng was impressed by his depth and regarded him as having accomplished the most of all of his students.

曹溪的弗昌——六祖云："得？"师曰："众角虽多，一麟足矣。"

溪，争知不失？"迁又问曰："曹溪大师还识和尚否？"师曰："汝今识吾否？"迁曰："识又争能识

师曰："将得什么来？"曰："未到曹溪亦不失。"师曰："恁么用去曹溪作什么？"迁曰："若不到曹

师言甚直，汝自迷耳。"迁闻语，便礼辞祖龛，直指静居。师问曰："子何方而来？"迁曰："曹溪来。"

奚为？"迁曰："我禀遗诫，故寻思尔。"第一座曰："汝有师兄行思和尚，今住吉州，汝因缘在彼，

何人？"祖曰："寻思去！"及祖顺世，迁每于静处端坐，寂若忘生。第一座问曰："汝师已逝，空坐

《景德传灯录》

Later, Xingsi was sent to Quingyuan Mountain in Ji prefecture to spread the dharma. There, he disseminated the orthodox teachings of Huineng.

He had only one outstanding disciple, Shitou Xiqian.

Although he was but one, he was sufficient. "Though horns are numerous, a unicorn suffices."

Xuanjue Of Yongjia
(665 ~ 713)

From Yongjia in Zhejiang province, his lay surname was Dai. He initially studied the Tiantai sect and was accomplished in meditation. Later he went to the place of Huineng to verify what he had learned.

1 At their first meeting, Xuanjue walked three circles around Huineng.

2 A monk should have three thousand kinds of dignified deportment and eighty thousand kinds of refined behavior.

Where are you from and why are you so bold and brash?

3 Life is but a breath. Everything changes so fast. How can I pay attention to it all?

4 If you're so worried about life, why don't you experience the great Dao, which transcends both rebirth and speed, and thereby be rid of all your troubles?

曹溪的佛唱——六祖坛经

研习，常修禅观。尝以见《维摩经》而发明心地。八岁出家，博探三藏，特通天台止观，与左溪玄朗为同门之友，住温州龙兴寺，寻自构禅庵，独居焉自坏。都捐我相，不污客尘。睹其寺旁，别有胜境，遂于岩下，自构禅庵。（中略）觉居其间也，丝不以衣，耕不以食。（下略）者，亦名僧也。并犹子二人，并预缁伍。觉本住龙兴寺，一门归信，连影精勤，定根确乎不移，疑树忽（中略）兄宣法师

唐温州龙兴寺玄觉禅师，字明道，俗姓戴氏，永嘉人也。总角出家，超年剃发。

《高僧传》

曹溪的弗唱——六祖坛经

门者，具三千威仪，八万细行，大德自何方而来，生大我慢？"祖曰："生死事大，无常迅速。"祖曰："夫沙弥轻，曹溪有六祖大师，四方云集，并是法者。"率师同往曹溪。初到，振锡携瓶，绕祖三匝。祖曰："夫沙门者，具三千威仪，八万细行，大德自何方而来，生大我慢？"师曰："生死事大，无常迅速。"祖曰："何不体取无生，了无速乎？"曰："体即无生，了本无速。"祖曰："如是，如是。"玄策方才作礼，须臾告辞。祖曰："返太速乎？"曰："本自非动，岂有速耶？"祖曰："谁知非动？"曰："仁者自生分别。"祖曰："汝甚得无生之意。"曰："无生岂有意耶？"祖曰："无意谁当分别？"曰："分别亦非意。"祖曰："善哉！"（以上录自《联灯会要》）

师曰："我听方等经论，各有师承，后于《维摩经》悟佛心宗，未有证明者。"策云："威音王以前即得，威音王以后，无师自悟，尽是天然外道。"师曰："愿仁者为我证据。"策云："我言轻，曹溪有六祖大师……"

The great Dao has neither beginning nor end, and the myriad things have no speed.

Well said, well said.
clap, clap, clap

Thank you for your instruction. I must take leave now.

Why must you go in such a hurry?

I haven't even moved. Why do you say I'm in a hurry?

40

Huizhong Of Nanyang
(677 ~ 775)

A native of Zhejiang province, Huizhong's lay surname was Ran. He was one of Huineng's five greatest disciples.

1 After studying under Huineng, he went to Baiya Mountain in Nanyang, where he lived for more than forty years, not once stepping foot off the mountain.

2 In the year 761, Emperor Suzong invited him to the capital to accept the post of National Teacher.

3 Once during a meeting with the emperor, although the emperor asked many questions, Huizhong refused to even look at him.

曹溪的佛唱——六祖坛经

闻岭表曹溪慧能禅师，盛扬法道，学者骏奔，乃效善财南方参问，裂裳裹足，以千里为跬步之间耳。法师下出家。其讽诵群经，易同反掌。全大律仪，匪贪讲贯。其《后汉书》，知浮图之说，由是于释教留神，乃无仕进之意。辞亲投本府国昌寺颢元老，灵府廓然。览

西京荷泽神会禅师，姓高，襄阳人也。年方幼学，厥性惇明，从师传授五经，克通幽赜；次寻庄

Shenhui Of Heze
(670 ~ 758)

From Xiangyang in Hubei province, Shenhui's lay surname was Gao. He made great strides in protecting Huineng's orthodoxy and in popularizing Zen. He also ensured that the Southern Sect of sudden enlightenment surpassed in popularity the Northern Sect of gradual enlightenment.

Shenhui first studied under Huineng when he was only thirteen.

Having come from so far away, did you bring your most fundamental thing?

1

If yes, you should know what its most important aspect is. See if you can tell me.

2

This thing of which you speak is non-abiding. It's most important aspect is opening one's eyes and seeing.

For such a young monk, you're pretty sharp.

3

Master, when you meditate, do you see or not?

4

bonk bonk bonk

5

When I hit you, does it hurt or not?

曹溪的佛唱——六祖坛经

行于秦洛。乃入京，天宝四年方定两宗，师寻往西京受戒。唐景龙中却归曹溪，乃著《显宗记》，盛行于世。祖灭后，二十年间，曹溪顿旨，沉废于荆吴，嵩岳渐门，盛诸佛之本原，神会之本性。」师礼拜而退。

他日，祖告众曰：「向汝道无头无尾，无名无字，汝便唤本原佛性。」

「各有一物，无头无尾，无名无字，无背无面，诸人还识否？」师乃出曰：「是诸知识，历劫难逢，今既得遇，岂惜身命。」自此给侍。

《景德传灯录》

曹溪的佛唱——六祖坛经

杀天下人。汝勿速说此法，病在汝身也。」马和尚在一处坐，让和尚将砖去面前石上磨，马师问：「作什么？」祖曰：「磨作镜。」马师曰：「磨砖岂得成镜邪？」「坐禅岂得成佛邪？」马师曰：「如何即是？」祖曰：「如人驾车不行，打车即是？打牛即是？」马师无对。祖又曰：「汝学坐禅，为学坐佛。若学坐禅，禅非坐卧。若学坐佛，佛非定相。於无住法，不应取舍。汝若坐佛，即是杀佛。若执坐相，非达其理。」马师闻示诲，如饮醍醐。礼拜问曰：「如何用心，即合无相三昧？」祖曰：「汝学心地法门，如下种子。我说法要，譬彼天泽。汝缘合故，当见其道。」又问曰：「道非色相，云何能见？」祖曰：「心地法眼能见乎道。无相三昧，亦复如是。」马师曰：「有成坏否？」祖曰：「若以成坏聚散而见道者，非见道也。听吾偈曰：『心地含诸种，遇泽悉皆萌，三昧华无相，何坏复何成？』」马师蒙开悟，心意超然。侍奉十秋，日益深奥。

（怀让）师乃往曹溪而依六祖，六祖问：「子近离何方？」对曰：「离嵩山，特来礼拜和尚。」祖曰：「什么物与摩来？」对曰：「说似一物即不中在。」祖曰：「还假修证不？」对曰：「修证即不无，不敢污染。」祖曰：「只此不污染，是诸佛之所护念。汝亦如是，吾亦如是。西天二十七祖般若多罗记汝，佛法从汝边云。向后，马驹踏

Dayi, Patriarch Ma (Mazu) (707~786)

From Chengdu in Sichuan province, his lay surname was Ma. Of all the Buddhist monks throughout history, he may be the only one to have gone by his lay surname.

Mazu left home to join the order at the young age of twelve. He went to Nanyu and took Huairang as his teacher.

The twenty-seventh patriarch of Indian Zen, Prajñātāra, prophesied that among your disciples there would be a strong horse (ma) that would range across the land.

After Huairang's enlightenment, Huineng once said to him:

48

曹溪的弗昌——六祖云经

以刀截发，投祖出家。

若教某甲自射，即无下手处。」祖曰：「遮汉旷劫无明烦恼，今日顿息。」藏当时毁弃弓箭，自射几个？」祖曰：「射一群。」曰：「彼此是命，何用射他一群？」曰：「一箭射一个。」祖曰：「汝不解射。」曰：「猎者。」祖曰：「汝解射否？」曰：「解射。」祖曰：「汝一箭射几个？」曰：「本以戈猎为务，恶见沙门，因逐鹿群，从马祖庵前过，祖乃逆之，藏问：「和尚见鹿过否？」祖

师曰：「飞过去也。」祖遂回头，将师鼻一挡，负痛失声。祖曰：「又道飞过去也！」师侍马祖行次，见一群野鸭飞过，祖曰：「是什么？」师曰：「野鸭子。」祖曰：「什处去也？」

《景德传灯录》

唐洪州百文山怀海禅师，福州长乐人也。早岁离俗，三学该练，属大寂阐化南康，乃倾心依附。与西堂智藏禅师，同号入室，时二大士为角立焉。

曹溪的佛唱——六且云经

老人遂于言下大悟，作礼云：「某甲已脱野狐身，住在山后，敢告和尚，乞依亡僧事例！」老人遂于言下大悟，作礼云：「不落因果！」五百生堕野狐身。今请和尚代一转语，贵脱野狐！」遂问：「大修行底人还落因果也无？」师曰：「不昧因果！」某甲对云：「不落因果！」五百生堕野狐身。今请和尚代一转语，贵脱野狐！」遂问：「大修行底人还落因果也无？」

百丈和尚凡参次，有一老人常随众听法，众人退，老人亦退，忽一日不退，师遂问：「面前立者复是何人？」老人云：「某甲非人也，于过去迦叶佛时，曾住此山。因学人问：『大修行

曹溪的佛唱——六祖坛经

朝参夕聚，饮食随宜，示节俭也；行普请法，示上下均力也。长老居方丈，同维那之一室也。不立刀睡，为其坐禅既久，略偃亚而已。又令不论高下，尽入僧堂，堂中设长连床，施椸架，挂搭道具。卧必斜枕床唇，谓之带刀睡。惟别院异耳。初自达摩传法，至六祖以来，得道眼者号长老，同西域道高腊长者，呼须菩提也，然多居律寺中，律，胡不依随乎？海曰：「吾于大小乘中，博约折中，设规务归于善焉。乃创意不循律制，别立禅居。」海且曰：「吾行大乘法，岂宜以诸部阿笈摩教为随行邪？」或曰：「《瑜伽论》，《璎珞经》，是大乘戒

Baizhang's Regulations

1 After Mazu died, Baizhang inherited the orthodox dharma.

2 He then established "Baizhang's Regulations", which became the foundation for the monastic order as well as Zen Buddhism in general.

3 Baizhang's Regulations set down in detail the rules for the daily life of the abbot and all those in the monastery under him.

4 And they required the prospective monk to vow to observe the Five Precepts:
- Do not kill
- Do not steal
- Do not be licentious
- Do not lie
- Do not drink

5 And the following:
Do not sleep on a high or broad bed
Do not observe or participate in stage shows
Do not adorn oneself
Do not acquire money or precious objects
Do not eat the wrong foods or at the wrong times

Only after achieving these would he formally have his head shaven and become a monk.

曹溪的佛唱——六祖坛经

不毁僧形，循佛制故；三、不扰公门，省狱讼故；四、不泄于外，护宗纲故。详此一条，制有四益：一、不污清众，生恭信故；二、不毁僧形，循佛制故；三、不扰公门，省狱讼故；四、不泄于外，护宗纲故。详此一条，制有四益：一、不污清众，生恭信故；二、不毁僧形，循佛制故，遵从偏门而出者，示耻辱也。或有所犯，即以拄杖杖之，集众烧衣钵道具，遣逐从偏门而出者，示耻辱也。或有所犯，即以拄杖杖之，集众烧衣钵道具，遣逐从偏门而出者，示耻辱也。或有所犯，即以拄杖杖之，集喧扰之事，即堂维那，检举抽下本位挂搭，摈令出院者，贵安清众也。或有假号窃形，混于清众，并别致其诸制度，与毗尼师，一倍相翻，天下丛林，如风偃草，禅门独行，由海之始也。佛殿，惟树法堂，表法超言象也。

《景德传灯录》

曹溪的弗唱——六祖坛经

逮，而帝终不悟。
国公者，着籍禁省，势倾公王。群居赖宠，更相凌夺。凡京畿上田美产，多归浮屠。虽藏奸宿乱踵相给。或夷狄入寇，必合众沙门诵护国仁王经为禳厌。幸其去，则横加锡与，不知纪极。胡人官至卿监封意向之，縠是禁中祀佛，引内沙门日百余，餼供珍滋，出入乘厩马，度支具禀所，讽令出财佐营作。初，代宗喜祠祀，而未重浮屠法，每从容问所以然，缙与元载盛陈福业报应。帝缙素奉佛，不茹荤食肉，晚节尤谨。妻死，以道政里第为佛祠。诸节度、观察使来朝，必邀至其

《新唐书·王缙传》

The Great Suppression

In the year 845 Buddhism in China was dealt a tragic blow when the Tang emperor Wuzong began a movement to wipe out Buddhism in China for reasons of economics.

For every man who doesn't farm, there are others who don't have food to eat. For every woman who doesn't weave, there are others who don't have clothes to wear. Yet the monasteries' monks and nuns neither farm nor weave, and the monasteries are rich and drain resources from the palace. This is what caused the fall of the Six Dynasties.

So more than 44,600 monasteries and temples were destroyed, more than 260,500 monks and nuns were returned to lay life, and over 15,000 servants were taken into service by the government.

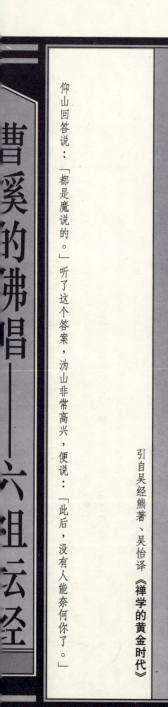

Congshen Of Zhaozhou
(778 ~ 863)

From Zi hill in Qing village, Zhaozhou's lay surname was Hao. When he was very young, he left home for the order at Longxing Monastery, and he took his vows at Song Mountain. Later, he went to Chi prefecture in Anhui province to study under Nanquan.

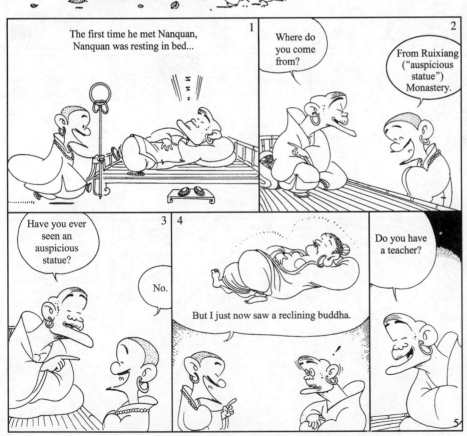

1. The first time he met Nanquan, Nanquan was resting in bed...
2. Where do you come from? — From Ruixiang ("auspicious statue") Monastery.
3. Have you ever seen an auspicious statue? — No.
4. But I just now saw a reclining buddha.
5. Do you have a teacher?

曹溪的佛唱——六祖坛经

「有主。」曰：「主在什么处？」师曰：「仲冬严寒，伏惟和尚尊体万福。」南泉器之，而许入室。
曰：「还见瑞像么？」师曰：「不见瑞像，只见卧如来。」曰：「汝是有主沙弥无主沙弥？」师曰：
（未具戒时）便抵池阳，参南泉，值南泉偃息，而问曰：「近离什么处？」师曰：「近离瑞像院。」
如。
龙兴伽蓝，从师剃落，寻往嵩山琉璃坛纳戒。师勉之听习于经律，但染指而已。闻池阳愿禅师，道化翕
唐赵州东院从稔禅师，青州临淄人也，童稚之岁，孤介弗群。越二亲之羁绊，超然离俗，乃投本州

73

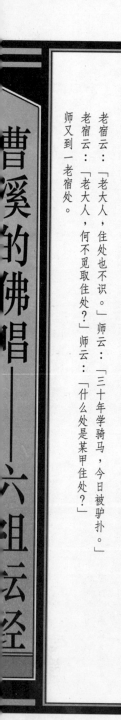

赛吧！

在所有的记载中，这是赵州第一次认输，也许这位老和尚当时很饿，为了得到饼，只好输了这场比

引自吴经熊著、吴怡译《禅学的黄金时代》

Daowu Of Tianhuang
(748 ~ 807)

From Dongyang in Zhejiang province, Daowu's lay surname was Zhang. He took his vows in Hang prefecture when he was twenty-five and then followed Daoqin of Jingshan, which was his first contact with Zen.

1. After following Jingshan for five years, he went to Mazu to verify his learning.

2. After two more years, he went to see Shitou Xiqian...

3. After one frees oneself of the concepts of meditation and knowledge, what other dharma is there to teach others?

There are no slaves here. What is this talk of freeing oneself?

4. I don't quite understand...

5. Do you understand emptiness?

6. This I've understood for a long time.

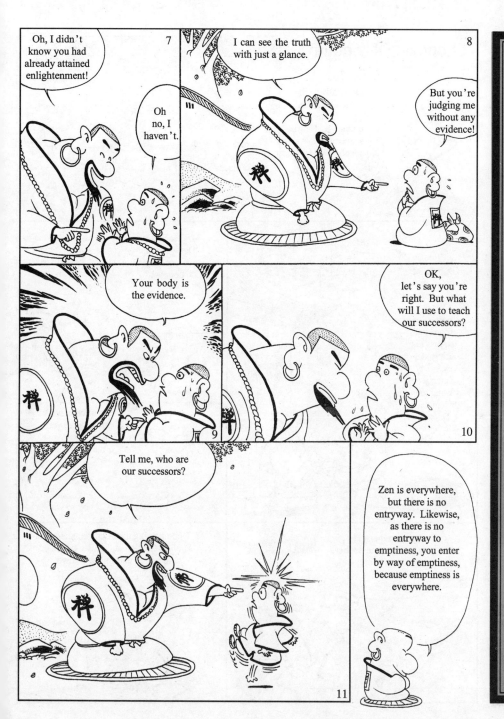

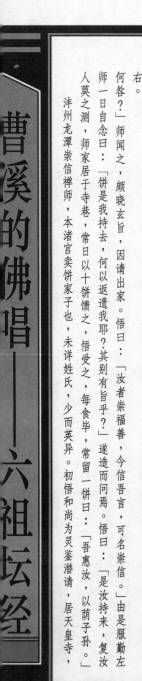

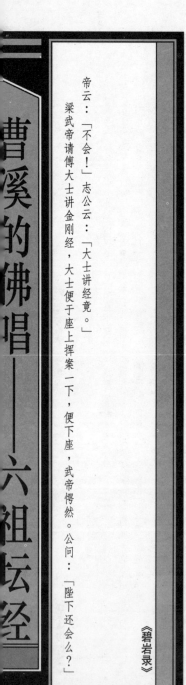

Liangjie Of Dongshan
(807 ~ 869)

From Huijin in Zhejiang province, Dongshan's lay surname was Yu. He joined the order as a boy, and after his enlightenment he became the abbot at Dong Mountain (Dongshan) in Jiangxi in the year 860. He was the founder of the Caodong (Sōtō) sect.

曹溪的佛唱——六祖云经

筠州洞山良价禅师，会稽人也，姓俞氏。幼岁从师，因念《般若心经》，以无根尘义问其师，其师骇异曰：「吾非汝师。」即指往五泄山，礼默禅师披剃。年二十一，嵩山具戒。游方首谒南泉，值马祖讳辰，修斋次，南泉垂问众僧曰：「来日设马师斋，甚堪雕琢。」师曰：「和尚莫压良为贼。」南泉乃出对曰：「待有是伴即来。」

次参沩山，问曰：「顷闻忠国师有无情说法，良价未究其微。」沩山曰：「我这里亦有，只是难得其人。」师曰：「某甲未明，乞师指示。」沩山竖起拂子，曰：「会么？」师曰：「不会，请和尚说。」沩山曰：「父母所生口，终不为子说。」

1. Once when he was a young monk, reciting the Heart Sūtra with his teacher... "No matter, no feeling, no thought, no action, no consciousness...."

2. "No idea of eyes, ears, nose, tongue, or body... no colors, sounds, smells, tastes..."

3. "I obviously have eyes, ears, nose, and a tongue, why does the scripture say I don't?"

4. "I think you should find another master. I'm not fit to teach you."

这个是。」师良久，云岩曰：「承当这个事，大须审细。」师犹涉疑，后因过水，睹影，大悟前旨，因又问云岩：「和尚百年后，忽有人问：『还貌得师真否？』如何只对？」云岩曰：「但向伊道，即自此一去难得相见。」师曰：「难得不相见。」曰：「莫归乡去？」师曰：「无。」曰：「早晚却来？」师曰：「待和尚有住处即来。」曰：「从此一别，难得相见。」曰：「难得不相见。」遂辞云岩，云岩曰：「什么处去？」师曰：「虽离和尚，未卜所止。」曰：「莫湖南去？」师曰：「无。」曰：「莫归乡去？」师曰：「无。」

若将耳听声不现，眼处闻声方可知。

Fayan Wenyi
(885 ~ 958)

From Yuhang in Zhejiang, Fayan's lay surname was Lu. As a boy, he left home to join the order and studied the dharma under the Vinaya master Xijue. He came to found the Fayan School, one of the five Zen schools.

1. Fayan traveled around the land, looking for guidance from various teachers. Once when he was passing by the Dicang Monastery, a snowstorm hit, and he stopped in to rest.

2. The monastery's abbot, Luohan Guichen, asked him: "Where are you going?" "I'm on a quest for understanding."

3. "Why a quest?" "I don't know."

4. "That's the best answer!"

5. "The snow has stopped. I should be going."

曹溪的佛昌——六祖云兰

（二）天台韶闻有僧问法眼云：「如何是曹溪一滴水？」法眼云：「是曹溪一滴水。」遂大悟。

（一）慧超问法眼云：「如何是佛？」法眼（清凉文益）云：「汝是慧超。」于言下大悟。

良苦，由此可见其一斑。举例如下：

说此句之用意，不像临济那样峻烈，而是以「应病与药」的手法去助人开悟，其用心良苦，由此可见其一斑。此种接引方法，不像临济那样峻烈，而是以「应病与药」的手法去助人开悟，其用心主要在于破斥别人法眼的宗风是「先利济」，中庸笃实。换句话说，就是用别人的话来回答别人

事见《人天眼目》

A Drop Of Water From the Cao River

离一切相的。在他眼中实体是空的，他和学生永明道潜的这段对话中便特别说明了这点。对华严经的造诣颇深，尤精于六相的原理和解释，但他却不认为现象界和实体界是同一的，因为实体是法眼是一位神秘论者，不过他的神秘不是在于自然和宇宙的不可知；而是在于其生生不已。虽然他

曹溪的佛唱——六祖坛经

Wenyan Of Yunmen
(864 ~ 909)

From Jiaxing in Zhejiang province, his lay surname was Zhang. He left home to join the order when very young, and his studies in the doctrines and discipline were excellent. In his later years he moved to the Guangtai Zen Monastery on Yunmen Mountain in Guangdong, where he promoted his own style of Zen. He was the founding master of the Yunmen school.

1. Yunmen once paid a visit to Muzhou, looking for guidance.

2. Who is it? / My name is Wenyan.

3. What are you here for? / I have yet to attain enlightenment, so I come for your guidance.

4. Muzhou opened the door, took one look, and then slammed the door shut.

5. For two days, Yunmen knocked on the door and was rejected. Then on the third day...

曹溪的佛唱──六祖坛经

韶州云门山光奉院文偃禅师，嘉兴人也，姓张氏。幼依空王寺志澄律师出家。敏质生知，慧辩天纵，及长落发，禀具于毗陵坛，侍澄数年，探穷律部。以已事未明，往参睦州，州才见来，乞师指示：「道！道！」州拟议，州便推出曰：「秦时𨍏轹钻。」遂掩门，损师一足。师从此悟入。

师乃扣门，州曰：「谁？」师曰：「某甲。」州曰：「作什么？」师曰：「已事未明，乞师指示。」州开门，一见，便闭却。师如是连三日扣门，至第三日，州开门，师乃拶入，州便擒住曰：「道！道！」师拟议，州便推出曰：

《指月录》

曹溪的佛唱——六祖云经

「一念不生，万法自泯。」问：「如何是涵盖乾坤？」答曰：「包裹太虚横贯三际。」问：「如何是截断众流句？」答曰：「随流得妙，应物全真。」问：「如何是随波逐流句？」答：「波逐流池也。」

本非解会，排叠将来，不消一字，万机顿息，即截断众流也。若许他相见，从苗辨地，因语识人，即随三句据圆悟勤的说法如下：「本真本空，一色一味，非无妙体，不在蹲踏，洞然明白，则涵盖乾坤也。此云门的主要代表人物为云门文偃。他以三句（涵盖乾坤、随波逐浪、截断众流）来接引修行人。此

图字:01-2005-2343

图书在版编目(CIP)数据

六祖坛经＝Wisdom of the Zen Masters:The Quest For Enlightenment/蔡志忠绘．—北京:现代出版社,2005
ISBN 7-80188-528-7

Ⅰ．六… Ⅱ．蔡… Ⅲ．漫画-作品集-中国-现代 Ⅳ．J228.2

中国版本图书馆 CIP 数据核字(2005)第 028133 号

Wisdom of the Zen Masters:The Quest For Enlightenment
六祖坛经:曹溪的佛唱

作者/〔台湾〕蔡志忠
译者/〔美〕Brian Bruya
总策划/吴江江
责任编辑/张　璐
封面设计/刘　刚
出版发行/现代出版社(北京安外安华里 504 号　邮编:100011)
印刷/北京平谷早立印刷厂
开本/880×1230　1/24　4 印张
版次/2005 年 5 月第 1 版
　　　2005 年 5 月第 1 次印刷
印数/1～6000 册
书号/ISBN 7-80188-528-7
定价/9.80 元